BRITAIN IN OLD PHOTOGRAPHS

THE OLD BOROUGH OF
SOUTHGATE

ALAN DUMAYNE

SUTTON PUBLISHING LIMITED

Sutton Publishing Limited
Phoenix Mill · Thrupp · Stroud
Gloucestershire · GL5 2BU

First published 1998

Copyright © Alan Dumayne, 1998

British Library Cataloguing in Publication Data
A catalogue record for this book is available from the
British Library.

ISBN 0 7509 2000 9

Typeset in 10/12 Perpetua.
Typesetting and origination by
Sutton Publishing Limited.
Printed in Great Britain by
Ebenezer Baylis, Worcester.

I dedicate this book to all kindred spirits interested in the local and social history of our area and to those societies that aim to foster and encourage this interest.

SOUTHGATE

OFFICIAL GUIDE

PRICE ONE SHILLING

Southgate's coat of arms shows a shield supported by two stags. On the shield is a gate over the rising sun. Surmounting all is the Minchenden Oak. The motto is *Ex Glande Quercus* – out of the acorn the oak.

CONTENTS

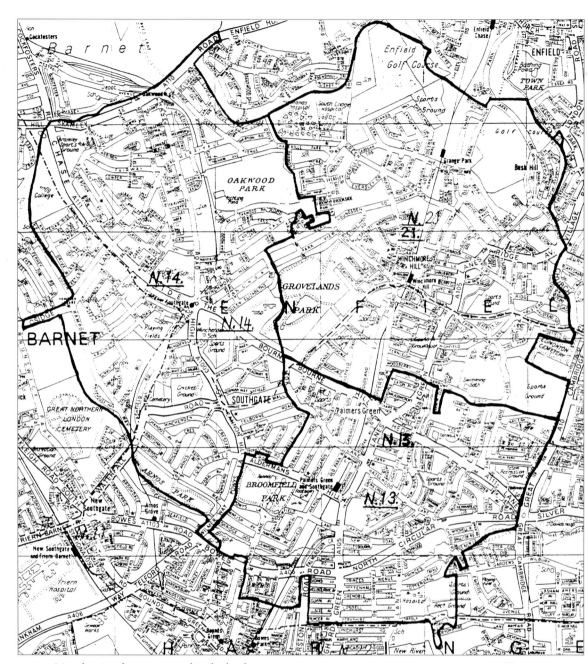

Map showing the area covered in this book.

INTRODUCTION

The Enfield book which I compiled for the Britain in Old Photographs series has proved to be so popular as to prompt a sequel, albeit in a slightly different format.

Having lived in the area all my life, the 'borough' that I knew as a boy and into manhood was Southgate, with its Town Hall situated in the Green Lanes in Palmers Green. The events leading up to the establishment of the borough are worth recording here.

Sir Ralph Littler was the last private tenant of Broomfield House, where he lived for twenty-five years. An eminent barrister, he masterminded the separation of Southgate (i.e. Southgate, Palmers Green and Winchmore Hill) from Edmonton in 1881. On 18 July 1881, with Royal Assent, Southgate's Local Board of Health was established. John Walker of Arnos Grove was the first chairman and the offices were in Ash Lodge on Southgate Green near the Cherry Tree. The house is still there. Southgate, Palmers Green and Winchmore Hill were now areas under new, more localised control.

Following the passing of the Local Government Act of 1894, Southgate became an Urban District, with a new Town Hall in Palmers Green. Southgate blossomed into full borough status on 30 September 1933 when Prince George, later the Duke of Kent, came to Arnos Grove in Cannon Hill (once the home of the great Walker family) to present the Charter of Incorporation. At that time the mansion served as the offices of the North Metropolitan Power Supply Company (Northmet House), later to become the headquarters of the Legal & General Assurance Company and currently divided into private apartments and a residential nursing home.

The Prince's visit was a truly momentous occasion, suitably celebrated, and, despite the intervention of war, it marked a period of optimism in the future and a feeling of pride among the growing number of residents in this attractive suburb. However, in 1965, along with many other boroughs, Southgate lost its independence and, once again, came under the control of a much larger administrative body – the London Borough of Enfield. The wheel had turned full circle.

In the 1980s, after years of research, I started to write about the history of the area I had grown to love. How to divide it, how to form my boundaries, proved difficult teasers. Rightly or wrongly I arrived at the answer: I would use the postal districts to determine my divisions. N14 would form my Southgate area, N13 Palmers Green and N21 Winchmore Hill. Reference to the maps contained in this book will assist you in following my method. The basis is far from perfect, for it excludes New Southgate (N11) and Cockfosters, both part of the former borough, but I have endeavoured to include these, where appropriate, by 'stretching' my boundaries.

In writing of the history I decided to start with *Southgate – A Glimpse into the Past* and I devised my chapter headings on the basis of a journey we would make within the N14 area. And so the seed was sown and similar guidelines were followed in subsequent publications, *Once Upon a Time in Palmers Green* and *Fond Memories of Winchmore Hill*.

I started to build up an extensive library of local history slides (some 2,500 to date) using photographs borrowed from various sources. First and foremost, I am most grateful to Graham Dalling, Local History Officer for the London Borough of Enfield, for his kind co-operation and support in allowing me access to his files and his knowledge. Secondly, I was becoming a collector of local photographs and postcards myself and these could be copied. Thirdly, many people through the years have kindly sent me photographs of the past from their own or inherited collections, allowing me to make my slides before returning the originals. May I make due acknowledgement to them and sincerely thank all my contributors. Their help and support is greatly appreciated.

My slide collection has required many years of patient endeavour, not only mastering the photographic processes, but also in keeping them catalogued, listed and boxed in logical order, but it has proved worthwhile for it has now become possible to reproduce them on the printed page.

As in my lectures, I have divided the three main areas into three parts — nine sections all told. Broadly speaking we go on a 'journey' as I have outlined in the text, and I have added a final section entitled 'Around & About' to give licence to include additional pictures that I hope will prove of interest.

This book is not fully comprehensive for, to give greater scope, I have tried to avoid repeating too many illustrations already published in my previous books. I have also endeavoured to make this more than just a 'picture book' by making the captions full and explanatory to assist readers in adding to their knowledge of this delightful area, the old borough of Southgate.

To many people, the name Southgate conjures up a Tube station near the end of the Piccadilly Line, but its origins go back into the mists of time. A tiny hamlet grew up where the five tracks met at the South Gate into Enfield Chase, a gate through which royal parties rode on horseback for their day's sport in this most beautiful of forests. All around, the area was one of great natural beauty with undulating hills and green fertile valleys. Brooks and streams ran their pleasant courses through farmers' fields and leafy woodland.

Please excuse my indulgence. I hope the pictures and my captions will add usefully to recording the history of our area.

ALAN DUMAYNE

The author Alan Dumayne died on 30 April 1998, shortly after he had completed work on this book. The following obituary appeared in the local press.

Alan Dumayne, who was born in Harringay, was a pupil at Highfield Road School, Winchmore Hill, moving on to the former Southgate County School in Palmers Green. Over the past 20 years he had helped to organise its reunions. At school Alan excelled at cricket and football. He went on to play football for Enfield and an Arsenal youth team, being selected to play for his county and country in representative matches. An injury put paid to a promising career.

When he left school he joined his father's building firm in south London. In 1980 he retired from business and took up fulltime writing, and achieved local fame by himself writing, publishing and marketing three best-selling hardback books, on the history of Palmers Green, Southgate and Winchmore Hill, which comprised the old Borough of Southgate and now form part of the London Borough of Enfield. Although these are now out of print, sales totalled more

Alan Dumayne 1929–1998

than 14,000 copies – a figure which most writers of non-fiction would be lucky to achieve nationally, let alone locally.

He was a painstakingly accurate writer, but he imbued his writing with the charm of constant personal references to places and people he had come to know and love as a lifelong resident. Alan painted scenes of other eras with an easy-flowing style, highlighting contrasts with today's environment. To many organisations, including schools, churches, Women's Institutes, Rotary Clubs, historical societies and libraries, Alan was above all a lively and compelling lecturer: by the time of his death, his talks had numbered nearly 400. They combined his talent for personal anecdote and photography, and included hundreds of slides of pictures he had taken himself.

In 1990 Alan became ill with leukaemia, a battle he fought successfully with a courage and determination which deeply impressed all who knew him.

As well as local history, his subjects included Sir Thomas Lipton, Lt Leefe-Robinson, who brought down the Cuffley Zeppelin, his own boyhood and teenage years, and London social history. He was a keen and active member of the Enfield Preservation Society, Southgate Civic Trust and the Edmonton Hundred Historical Society. He was also a vice-president of Southgate Compton Cricket Club and a player with Grovelands Bowling Club.

Alan leaves a widow, Sheila, to whom he had been happily married for 45 years, a son, Richard, a daughter, Jackie, and three grandchildren.

CHAPTER ONE

SOUTHGATE

PART ONE: THE CIRCUS TO OAKWOOD

In our journey around Southgate we start at Fiveways, the heart of the old village, often known as Bunkers Corner before the turn of the century. It was here that George Bunker set up in business as a wheelwright and ironworker in 1804 in a large, rambling, clapboarded building. The premises were demolished in 1897 and were replaced by some shops; the shops later made way for the Tube station. We look at The Grange before travelling up Chase Side, with reference to Sir Thomas Lipton of Osidge and Charles Baring Young of Oakhill. We then turn right into Bramley Road, once a country lane giving access to three farms and, further on, South Lodge. The Tube arrived at Enfield West (subsequently renamed Oakwood) in 1933, which prompted extensive development over the once green and open countryside.

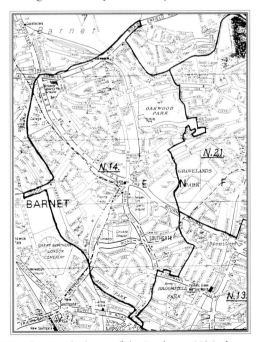

Map showing the limits of the Southgate, N14, district.

J. Furse, butchers, *c.* 1900. The shop stood on the south side of Chase Side, near the Fiveways junction. Along with many other shops, it was sacrificed for the coming of the Tube in 1933, with the formation of Southgate Circus. In days of yore, the butchers took great pride in displaying their locally killed carcasses, though today the Environmental Health Officer would no doubt object.

Conisbee, the bakers, was founded in 1830 and was situated on the north side of Chase Side, near Fiveways. The Conisbee family were well known in the village, one member, William, being the builder responsible for Conisbee Cottages in Chase Road. Conisbee Court gives access to some maisonettes, built on what were the cottages' back gardens.

Looking due north. The shop advertising 'Refreshments & Teas' is one of a block later demolished to make way for Southgate Circus. The lovely triangle of trees likewise met its fate. The building far distance left is The Bell, one of Southgate's oldest inns, which stood on the corner with Chase Road before it made way for development in 1963.

These shops, photographed in about 1905, stood on the south side of Chase Side and were very much part of the village scene until their demolition in the early 1930s, to make way for Southgate Circus. Note the brick-built shops (left), standing alongside the more typical clapboarded cottages of the period.

The Grange, built in 1875 on the corner of The Bourne and High Street, will always be associated with John Bradshaw, who lived there from 1895 until his death in December 1939. In 1906, after the death of his uncle, V.E. Walker of Arnos Grove, John had become President and Chairman of Taylor Walker, the brewers. The demolition of the house and the subsequent redevelopment caused much controversy in post-war years.

An aerial view of Southgate looking north-west from The Bourne is of interest, showing various landmarks. The Odeon cinema can be seen in the foreground on the right, opposite the Grange site on the corner with High Street. Southgate Circus looks clean and tidy, with Crown Lane and Chase Side going off into the distance. If only the traffic were as light today!

The work is going ahead in 1931 with the construction of Southgate Circus in preparation for the arrival of the Tube. The Bell pub stands on the corner of Chase Road, with the barber's shop next door. The hoardings in Winchmore Hill Road herald the building of a new block of shops, later known as Dennis Parade.

The Circus has been built and the Tube is on the way. Note Conisbee, the baker's shop with the Hovis sign on the wall (see page 10). As with all these early scenes, the absence of traffic is immediately apparent. How times have changed!

The year is 1933 and the work is complete. The Tube has arrived, all is pristine and new, and the roads are still uncluttered. Development was now under way in earnest.

Looking east down The Bourne, 1931. The shops, including United Dairies, are all ready to serve us and the Odeon cinema is due to open in late October. The boundary wall of The Grange can be seen, right, and John Bradshaw is still in residence. There is not a yellow line or a traffic warden to be seen.

Chase Side looking towards Fiveways. At the turn of the century, Southgate was still a quiet country village. Though Chase Cycle Works have ceased trading, the high gabled flank wall can still be identified today and the single-storey building, once a café, is currently an estate agent's premises. The cottages, left foreground, have been replaced by a modern shopping parade.

The Rising Sun in Chase Side has changed dramatically since this picture was taken. Frank Lowe was the licensee who ran a local horsebus service from here to Colney Hatch station, a useful link for the villagers into Kings Cross but, after 1871 and the extension of the Great Northern Railway, the service switched to serve the new Palmers Green station.

In 1898 John Eaton was the village jobmaster and coachmaster in Chase Side. Always immaculately turned out, he hired out every type of horse-traffic conveyance imaginable and, as motorised transport was introduced, he hired out Daimlers and became an agent for man's new invention, the motor car. It was quite a transformation.

Southgate's 'Beggars Bush Fair' was established early in the seventeenth century in the fields between the Crown and the Rising Sun. Originally Bush Fairs were established for the purpose of hiring servants, but they soon became associated with the swings, roundabouts and sideshows that are more familiar today. Having been part of village life for 300 years, the fair petered out around 1912.

I am indebted to the artist George Downing who made this delightful sketch of some cottages in Crown Lane in 1932, 'sitting in a tree on a warm summer's day' when he was just twenty. With the opening of the Tube the following year, this scene would soon be lost forever. The thatched cottages were close to where the Police Station stands today.

Tommy Lipton (1850–1931), born in Glasgow of Irish parents, lived the last thirty-eight years of his life in Southgate. A man of immense energy and flair, he started with nothing and achieved so much in setting up his grocery empire, competing five times in the Americas Cup and becoming the friend and confidant of royalty.

Tommy Lipton was knighted in 1898. He often visited America, which he was proud to call his second home. In spite of successive failures in the Americas Cup, the American people warmed to his character and he became a celebrity. This picture was taken at a rodeo in the USA and also features Tom Mix (far left) and Jack Dempsey (centre).

The grounds of Sir Thomas Lipton's Osidge estate featured a footpath which traversed his grounds, part of a lovely country walk that was popular with the old villagers. The path emerged into a country lane, now known as Osidge Lane, at this trysting stile, situated very close to where Hampden Square is today.

Ferney Lodge in Osidge Lane, *c*. 1900. A lovely picture of a quiet country lane before the development of the 1930s. We are looking east, up to what is now Hampden Square. The Lodge, which was at the entrance to Ferney House, was demolished in 1932 and the site is now a pizza shop, though many will remember the fried fish shop that preceded it.

Charles Baring Young of Oakhill devoted much of his life and wealth to looking after the welfare of the poor and deprived working-class lads of London. An untiring philanthropist, he died in 1928 and, in accordance with his wishes, Oakhill became a theological college and remains so to this day.

The South Lodge estate extended into Enfield territory in the extreme north-east corner of our region and comprised over 120 acres when it was purchased in 1935 by John Laing for redevelopment. The old house is mentioned in the parish register as early as 1616. Set in most glorious countryside with ponds and trees adding to its beauty, the house was latterly used as a school, prior to closure at the end of the summer term, 1935.

Looking north up Chase Road to the Bramley Road junction, 1932. Eastpole Farm, facing us, has not much longer to survive for the Tube is on the way, and is to be extended northwards as far as Cockfosters. The site of Enfield West station (later renamed Oakwood) can be clearly seen, then in the midst of beautiful countryside.

CHAPTER TWO

SOUTHGATE

PART TWO: OAKWOOD TO THE HIGH STREET

From Oakwood we turn south down Chase Road to Southgate Circus, to the very spot where the South Gate into Enfield Chase had stood. We look at some of the roads that once radiated from the old Fiveways junctions: Winchmore Hill Road, once just a country lane that led to the Chase Side Tavern; The Bourne, which leads us to an entrance to Grovelands and up the hill to The Woodman; and back to the High Street, where we journey on towards Ye Olde Cherry Tree.

Gwalior House in Chase Road, 1936, a year before its demolition to make way for a block of flats which still bears the name. It was to be the home of a much loved couple, Lt General J.D. Campbell of the Royal Engineers and his wife Harriet, who sadly died just before its completion in 1882. The General had served with great distinction, in particular at Gwalior at the time of the Indian Mutiny, and he chose to name his house in memory of that campaign.

Lt General Campbell served with distinction at the battle of Maharajpur, at Gwalior and in the Second Burmese War. His wife Harriet, always known to the villagers as 'Lady' Campbell, was the heroine at Gwalior when, in the face of great danger, she led a party of women and children to safety. After his retirement, the General built Gwalior House but, after the death of his partner, he became a recluse until his death in 1885.

Oak Lodge Farm (originally known as Chase Farm) was owned latterly by one of the big landowners of the district, Samuel Sugden, who lived nearby at Oak Lodge. The farm was situated in Chase Road, opposite Avenue Road. The track in the foreground is now Merrivale and today the Piccadilly Line crosses the field in the distance.

Oak Lodge was the home of Mr and Mrs Sugden and their three daughters. They owned much of the land on the east side of Chase Road. After Samuel's death in 1905, the estate was gradually disposed of, some for development and some to Southgate Council to form the nucleus of Oakwood Park. This picture of some of the outbuildings shows the ice well which can still be identified today.

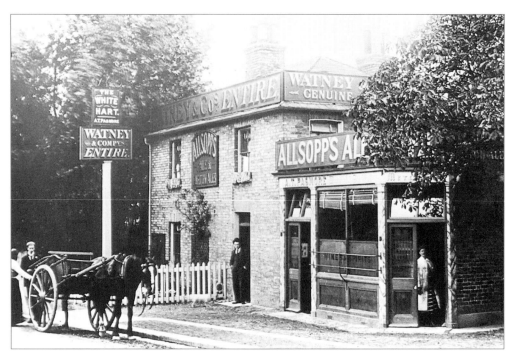

The White Hart stood on the east side of Chase Road, just before the Fiveways junction. It is still there today but in a slightly different guise. Once there were no fewer than six licensed premises within a stone's throw of our village centre. The horse and cart indicates a more leisurely period of our history, before the arrival of the motor car.

Looking down Winchmore Hill Road from Fiveways, 1922. There is not a car to be seen. The brick boundary wall of the Queen Elizabeth Lodge estate can just be seen on the right. A complete transformation was to come in the 1930s, with the arrival of the Tube and the creation of the new shopping parades.

Burrows Cottages were built in 1852 on the north side of Winchmore Hill Road. Hope Cottage (right) became the home of Robert Blagden (Principal of the Academy, on the corner of Blagdens Lane) on his retirement in 1857. The site is now occupied by a block of flats, Lauder Court, on the corner with St Thomas Road.

Winchmore Hill Road was once just a country lane. The south side was completely rural and tree lined, being part of Taylor's Grovelands estate. On the north side (pictured here in 1882) lay Simmons' ice well and Taylor's Home Farm, all later to be developed with the creation of The Vale and the extensive Laing estate of the 1930s.

Winchmore Hill Road was once called Chase Side for it bordered the renowned Enfield Chase which stretched northwards as far as Potters Bar. In this picture, as we approach the Tavern, the scene is still rural. There are some dwellings to be seen on the left, but the land opposite remains part of the Grovelands estate, as yet undeveloped.

The Odeon cinema in The Bourne, which opened in October 1931, was always very popular in the age before television. The marvellous films of the 1930s, '40s and '50s played to packed houses night after night. In the '60s, audiences began to dwindle, and the doors closed in September 1972. It later reopened as a small, privately run cinema – stalls only – but the final curtain came in January 1981.

This lovely print shows the house that Mr Walker Gray had built in 1797–8, which he called Southgate Grove. John Nash was the architect and Humphry Repton the landscape gardener. In 1835, after the death of Walker Gray, the house and estate were bought by his nephew, John Donnithorne Taylor, who renamed it Grovelands. The eventual sale of his estate in 1902 triggered the start of development in the area.

Grovelands was used as an auxiliary hospital for wounded soldiers during the First World War, and many fetes and fund-raising activities took place to assist in its upkeep. It continued to serve as a public hospital until 1977, and then remained empty for several years. In 1986, reinstated to its former glory, it reopened as Grovelands Priory Hospital for patients suffering from mental and addiction problems.

John Donnithorne Taylor was the major landowner in the area for most of the nineteenth century. He lived at Grovelands from 1835 until his death fifty years later and, during his lifetime, he fought hard to resist the spread of London out to these northern reaches. He refused to allow the property developers their way and strenuously opposed the extension of the railway in 1871. He had close links with the Walker family, both by marriage and in business (i.e. the Taylor Walker brewery).

A lovely old picture of Bourne Hill looking up to the Woodman, with the village pound in the distance at the junction with Fox Lane. The year is 1883 and the scene is completely rural. The Woodman started life as a country cottage in 1727 before Henry Wale, a retired police sergeant, was granted a licence to serve ale in 1868.

In this view we are looking west from the Woodman towards Southgate, as the pony and trap struggles up the slope towards us. The winding lane has since been straightened into a busy thoroughfare, with the almost incessant traffic rushing by.

Sir John Lawrence, seen here, became a tenant at Southgate House in the High Street in 1862. The estate was then still owned by the Walker family, who had moved on to Arnos Grove in Cannon Hill. On being appointed Viceroy of India in 1864, Sir John left to take up his duties, his wife and family joining him the following year, leaving his sister, Letitia Hayes, in residence.

Southgate High Street, looking north. Seen here at the turn of the century, it represents a different world, as the haycarts trundle by.

James Henry Leigh Hunt, poet, author and critic, was born in 1784 at Leigh Lodge in the High Street, Southgate. As a young man of eighteen, his first collection of verses received great acclaim. He became close friends with many of his great literary contemporaries. In 1813 he was imprisoned for writing a derogatory article in *The Examiner*, criticising the Prince Regent (later George IV), but his career continued to prosper. He later moved to Hampstead, where he died in 1859.

Mr Lyne's butcher's shop, 1870. This was situated on the west side of High Street, nearly opposite the Woolpack inn. He would undoubtedly have had great pride in this display of fresh meat, all locally produced on the nearby farms.

Photographed in 1890, the Shakespeare Cottages were typical of an old-fashioned High Street in a country village – the front clad in greenery, a small attractive front garden with picket fence, and a general air of tranquillity. They survived for over 200 years prior to demolition and the erection of a modern block of maisonettes, which bears the name Shakespeare House.

CHAPTER THREE

SOUTHGATE

PART THREE: THE GREEN TO ARNOS GROVE

On the Green, Ye Olde Cherry Tree is a good place to start, whence we travel south down Cannon Hill into Powys Lane and Wilmer Way. On our return journey we pause to look at Arnos Grove, the old Walker home. From the Green we now turn west along Waterfall Lane, down to the bridge. We cross into New Southgate territory (N11) and climb the hill to join up with Bowes Road, and witness another reminder that the Tube is on the way.

Ye Olde Cherry Tree is one of the oldest inns in the area and is thought to date from the late sixteenth century.
It is the centrepiece for Southgate Green, around which a tiny hamlet called South Street became established. It became a post coach inn, where the horses would be stabled overnight ready for the coachmen, suitably refreshed, to resume their journey north the next morning. Note the footpath, right of the inn, which existed before the creation of The Mall.

We see evidence of the shops that used to trade on the north side of the inn. Beyond is the ivy-clad home of Revd Benjamin Waugh, founder of the NSPCC. This was later converted into a bank but was subsequently demolished to make way for a new branch, which opened in 1927. In recent years, Barclays have left and the building is now used as a nursery school. Sandford House and Norbury House feature in the distance.

We see more evidence of the lovely Georgian row of cottages at the Cherry Tree, still trading as shops in 1962 when this photograph was taken. On the extreme left, at the end of the terrace, is the 'new' Barclays Bank referred to above. The motor car is beginning to make its presence felt.

The modern parade of shops, on the south side of The Mall corner, dates from 1933 but, prior to their development, this delightful pair of dwellings, photographed in 1908, stood roughly where the 'gap' into the motor car workshops exists today. The elegant house on the left was called Lawn Side, with Bay Tree Cottage alongside, notable for its distinctive turret-like roof at one corner.

The Cherry Tree, looking north. This is from a postcard postmarked 1910, though the photograph may pre-date it. A lovely rural scene with a greensward of trees, and only a horse and cart to disturb the peace of a sunny Sunday afternoon.

Looking south down Cannon Hill, 1922. Aldermans Hill joins to the left and Powys Lane is straight ahead. It is a different world: the road surface is unmade, no traffic lights are needed, and an onlooker gazes into the distance. On the right, where Forestdale now joins, are some cottages where workers on the Arnos Grove estate once lived.

The Wilmer Way bridge over Pymmes Brook in 1929. Wilmer Way is a modern road constructed after the departure of Lord Inverforth from Arnos Grove. The road is fully developed now, a busy thoroughfare linking up with the North Circular Road. The contrast with yesteryear, as we look west in this picture across open countryside, is plain to see.

In this delightful picture of Powys Lane, looking north, we are again reminded of another era and a much slower pace of life. The 'lane' is named after the Powys family who lived at Broomfield House from the beginning of the nineteenth century. They set about improving the roads around the estate and thus their name has endured.

As we return to the Green, we look in at Arnos Grove, the home of the Walker family from 1777 to 1918. Their influence on village life was considerable and spanned four generations. The last of these, comprising five daughters and seven sons, had special appeal and charisma. Lord Inverforth took over in 1918 for ten years, before his move to Hampstead, when the estate was developed and Arnos Park was created.

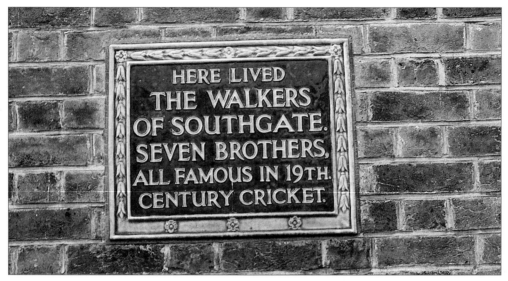

This simple plaque tells its tale. The Walkers of Southgate and their contribution to our game of cricket cannot be overstated. The seven sons were all fine county players and the annual matches between the village and the All England XI, on what is now called the Walker Ground, have passed into folklore. The sons were also very involved with the administration of the game and the establishment of the Middlesex County HQ at Lords in 1877.

The haybarn, Arnos Grove, 1926. In 1862 the Weld Chapel was demolished and Christ Church was built in Waterfall Lane. The Walker family carefully preserved the bell turret and weather vane from the chapel and had them erected over the haybarn on their estate. When the barn was eventually demolished, the turret crumbled to dust, but the weather vane can still be seen above a garage workshop in Palmers Green.

Our journey down Waterfall Lane starts here, with this view looking west from the Green, *c.* 1900. The Duchess Pond, seen here, was named in memory of the Duchess of Chandos, who lived at the big house nearby called Minchenden. In the distance stands Christ Church, a fine example of Sir George Gilbert Scott's design, a landmark for miles around.

Chapel Fields, now known as the Walker Ground and home of Southgate CC. The fields had long been the centre for the villagers' sporting activities and celebrations. John, the eldest of the Walker brothers, spent large sums on returfing the ground and founded the cricket club in 1855. For miles around, Southgate was soon to become the mecca of cricket.

Southgate Cycling Club on Chapel Fields, 1902. The club, founded in 1886, is thought to have been one of the oldest established cycling clubs in the country. Several well-known villagers are included in this picture. The central figure (bearded) is V.E. Walker. Apart from his great prowess as a cricketer, he was a tower of strength to the community, and his death in 1906 was a great blow to the village.

The entrance lodge and drive into the Beaver Hall estate was on the south side of Waterfall Lane, nearly opposite the cemetery. The drive entered through attractive grounds and swept round to the hall, with picturesque views over the Pymmes Brook valley.

This print clearly shows the ideal position of Beaver Hall with its glorious outlook. It was the birthplace and home of Henry Schneider, who was instrumental in setting up the Barrow Iron & Steel Works. Note the ha-ha around the grounds. In 1870 John Walker bought the estate and demolished the Hall, the site of which is now 41–49 Chandos Avenue.

These are the arches in Arnos Park that form the viaduct constructed in the early 1930s. They are needed to carry the Tube railway across the Pymmes Brook valley, and are a magnificent example of the bricklayer's craft of this era. There are thirty-four (numbered) arches spanning the park, followed by Waterfall Lane bridge. Then four more arches connect to the Hampden Way bridge. Thereafter, the embankment runs on the surface before disappearing underground, just before Southgate Tube station.

The Waterfall Lane bridge spanning Pymmes Brook, 1906. A horse and cart wends its way down the hill from The Green and a young lad pauses to look at the camera. Nature's beauty is all around.

Why Waterfall Lane you may ask? Looking upstream, this modest drop in the flow of Pymmes Brook hardly warrants its title 'The Waterfall', as printed on the old maps, but thus the lane was christened. The 'lane' is now officially a 'road', but do not mention this to any locals of long standing as they, like the author, prefer the original title.

A lovely day for a walk down Waterfall Lane in the quiet countryside, *c.* 1900. There are no pavements, kerbstones or lighting, but then there is no traffic. This view is taken from the New Southgate end, with the Arnos Grove estate to our right.

Looking south, in 1925, towards the junction which was always known as Lander's Corner (after A.K. Lander, the monumental masons who traded there). The latest sports car catches our eye and, in the distance on the right, we can see the pointed turret of the Clock & Watchmakers' Asylum.

The Clock & Watchmakers' Asylum was built on the corner of Brunswick Park Road in 1858. The word 'asylum' means 'place of refuge' in this context and the homes, supervised by a warden, provided accommodation and sustenance for those retired from the profession. It was a fine early example of a trade looking after its members. The buildings were demolished in the 1950s to make way for flats.

The year is 1931, the Tube is on the way and the board goes up with some suggested names. The locals still had fond memories of the Arnos Grove estate, the Walker family and Lord Inverforth, the last private owner. The station was to be built on the southern extremity, with the line traversing the estate. 'Arnos Grove' it had to be.

CHAPTER FOUR

PALMERS GREEN

PART ONE: HAZELWOOD LANE TO FIRS LANE

The centre of the old village of Palmers Green was the Village Stores, on the corner of
Hedge Lane and Green Lanes, and it is here that we start our journey. We cross to the Fox
Inn and Skinners' Almshouses opposite and progress up Fox Lane, towards the Woodman.
We change direction here to travel down Dog & Duck Lane (Bourne Hill), before crossing
Green Lanes into Hedge Lane. Then a brief look at Firs Lane and it is time to rest.

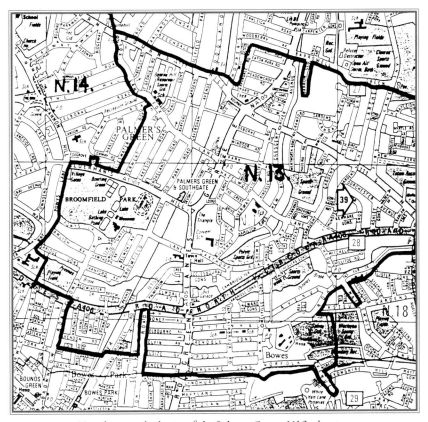

Map showing the limits of the Palmers Green, N13, district.

The heart of the old village, at the junction of Hazelwood Lane and Green Lanes. The Village Stores is on the corner with Perrins, the boot and shoe repairers, next door. A few clapboarded cottages still straggle down the lane, but change is on the way. The tramway has arrived along Green Lanes and development has begun.

The same corner as above, but the year is 1933. The Village Stores and the clapboarded cottages have gone. The National Provincial Bank and a modern block of shops leading up to the new Post Office now feature in Green Lanes. Note, too, the tramlines in the roadway with a tram approaching.

Palmers Green was a tiny village set in a farming community when, in 1878, the Knight family set up an independent mission in two cottages in Hazelwood Lane. As time went by, the Baptists and the Congregationalists came to worship here. In the early 1900s, with the sudden influx of new residents, the chapel adapted to their needs before the new churches could be funded. The cottages are the site of the Pilgrims Rest.

An historic picture of the first tram to run along Green Lanes in 1907. The new tramway was extended from Manor House and reached the Green Dragon that year, hastening the development already under way, following the sale of the Taylor estates. The new Fox Hotel can be seen, built in 1904 to replace its humble predecessor, and the presence of a roadsweeper bears out the transformation.

The old Fox was a delightful inn, the original local in a sleepy country village. On warm summer days, drinks would be served through the open windows to the customers outside, making use of the forms and tables provided. In 1904 the new Fox inn was built to serve a growing population.

THE FOX STORES, GREEN LANES, PALMERS GREEN,
Established **200 YEARS.**
ALL HIGH CLASS WINES & SPIRITS. BEERS & MINERAL WATERS
THE BEST GUARANTEED BRANDS
ALL Goods Supplied of the Best Quality.
FAMILIES WAITED UPON DAILY. = PROMPT DELIVERY GUARANTEED.
Arthur Davey. Proprietor.

I DESIRE TO DRAW your special attention to my
SPECIAL BRAND D.O. WHISKEY,
The Best Value In The Market, AND STILL SOLD
AT **3/6** PER BOT. OLD. MELLOW. & UNIFORM QUALITY.
ONCE TASTED NEVER CHANGED.

This advertisement offers the best scotch whisky for 3s 6d per bottle. The landlord at the time was Arthur Davey, whose family had managed the inn both before and after the rebuild of 1904. Arthur was born at The Fox in 1867. He was highly respected and served as a local councillor for eighteen years. He died in 1932. The family connections with the inn spanned 225 years.

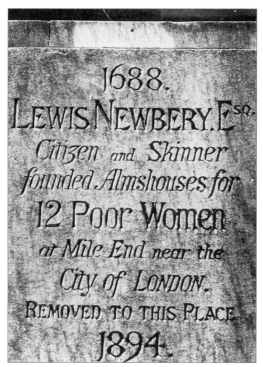

The Skinners' Almshouses, on the corner of Green Lanes and Fox Lane, were built in 1894 on what had once been Mr Graves' farm. This plaque at the entrance told us of their origins. Of most attractive design, they were a well-known feature of the village, which later grew into a suburb. Local residents were saddened, in 1966, when they were destroyed by fire. The redevelopment includes a private access road, blocks of flats and some new almshouse units.

On 6 December 1912 a light aircraft piloted by Mr Jean de Manio (father of Jack, the broadcaster) made an emergency landing on the roof of 75 Derwent Road. Two boys from Southgate County School (Cecil Hunt and Arthur Wiggins) were having tea in a house opposite. Hearing the crash, they ran back to school to fetch a ladder and then mounted a successful rescue operation.

The picturesque Fir Tree Cottage, seen here in 1881, was situated near the top of Fox Lane, then just a quiet country lane surrounded by farmland. It was demolished in 1912 to make way for the new church (next picture) which, in turn, has made way for Lady Shaw Court, situated just above the old Southgate County School buildings (since converted into apartments).

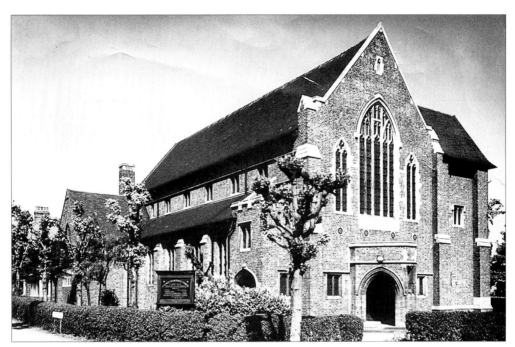

Fir Tree Cottage was demolished in 1912 and work began on the building of St George's Presbyterian Church, pictured here. In 1972 the merger took place, nationally, between the Congregational and Presbyterian Churches to create the United Reformed Church. With both faiths having fine buildings in Fox Lane and good local support, there was much debate to decide which church should stay and which should go. This church disappeared in 1980.

Clappers Green Farm was the centre of a tiny hamlet situated at the top of Fox Lane. The farm, a most attractive mixture of arable and pasture land, hedges and trees, was triangular in plan with the apex at the junction of Fox Lane and Dog & Duck Lane (Bourne Hill), and the base being the railway line parallel to Green Lanes. It was sold in 1908 and was immediately developed with roads and housing.

The Southgate area abounded in wells, which were a very important feature of village life before mains water became available. This delightful picture, *c.* 1900, shows the well situated almost opposite the Woodman, which once supplied the needs of the inn and the nearby cottages.

As we turn to head east down Dog & Duck Lane, on our left was the stile into Winchmore Woods. The stile marks today's entry into Broad Walk, which follows the line of the old footpath that led to The Green. This old villager was exercising his right to collect kindling wood from the forest for his fire.

These old cottages stood in Dog & Duck Lane, long before motorised traffic was ever dreamed of. The lane originally led to the inn of that name in Hoppers Road, which still exists (rebuilt 1900), and the new bridge has been built to accommodate the ever-increasing demands of the traffic (see below).

Bourne Hill originally met Hoppers Road opposite the Dog & Duck at a 90° junction which, in turn, fed into Green Lanes. However, this became a main route for heavy traffic to connect up with the A10 and North Circular Road and, accordingly, a new 'skew' bridge was built in 1971 to ease and withstand the traffic flow. The Telephone Exchange building can be seen in the background.

Poet and novelist Stevie Smith (1902–71) is well remembered in Palmers Green. She was born in Hull but, at the age of three, came to live in Avondale Road, originally with her mother and later on with her 'Lion Aunt'. A commemorative plaque marks her home. She was a contemporary of Flora Robson (see page 127), both attending Palmers Green High School in Green Lanes and in Hoppers Road. In 1997 her life story was featured on television.

It is not difficult to see why it was called Hedge Lane. In 1927 when this picture was taken, there were no pavements or lighting, no kerbstones or proper road surface. It was just a track for the haycarts to wend their way between the hedges, down to Huxley Farm, situated where Ash Grove lies today.

Firs Lane, looking south towards Hedge Lane, 1910. This whole area remained a farming community into the 1930s. An artist captures the rural scene, showing Bunce's Farm with barns adjoining. The roof of Myrtle Cottage, once the home of J.T. Smith, a fine engraver, can just be seen. The area is now fully developed with a shopping 'square' left of picture.

CHAPTER FIVE

PALMERS GREEN

PART TWO: ST MONICA'S CHURCH TO BOWES MANOR

St Monica's Church and its hall, which became the Intimate Theatre, is the most northerly point of the parish and we proceed due south down Green Lanes with memories of the marvellous shops and cinemas. We go past the Triangle and the Town Hall, down to the old Cock Inn. We look at Tile Kiln Lane which, before the North Circular Road came into being, provided an important link with Edmonton. We rest awhile in the lovely grounds of Bowes Manor.

Though out of sequence, I had to include this lovely old print of the Triangle, date unknown. Green Lanes was originally a drover's track with trees and fields lining the route. The cattle could be driven southwards down to London's meat market, Smithfield, which then had its own abattoirs. We are looking north here, with Aldermans Hill joining to the left.

Sir John Clements, star of stage and screen, will long be associated with the Intimate Theatre in Palmers Green. Originally built as the Parish Hall of St Monica's Church, he took it over in 1935 when forming his own repertory company. Up to 1940, Sir John appeared in 200 plays there, most of which he directed. The theatre suffered in post-war years with the competition of television and closed in 1988, just prior to his death. The hall is still used occasionally for public performances.

With development rapidly going ahead in Palmers Green, it was obvious that a major new church would soon be required. The Revd John Beardall, vicar of Christ Church in Waterfall Lane, prompted a start, aided by the generosity and foresight of V.E. Walker and his sister, Anna Baird. 'V.E.W.' laid the foundation stone on 17 October 1903 and, in January 1906, St John's was assigned its own parish.

As Palmers Green started to develop, the Post Office was moved, in 1904, from Hazelwood Lane to Lacey's shop at the Triangle. In 1907 a new Sorting Office (seen here) was built in Green Lanes opposite Fox Lane. This arrangement continued until 1931, when the Sorting Office was demolished to make way for the new integral Post Office, which opened on 1 January 1932.

In its heyday, Palmers Green was noted for its shops, some of which can be seen here in the 1950s. Points to note are the trolleybus wires overhead and the almost complete absence of traffic. Pedestrians stroll across the road unhampered, and yellow lines are nowhere to be seen.

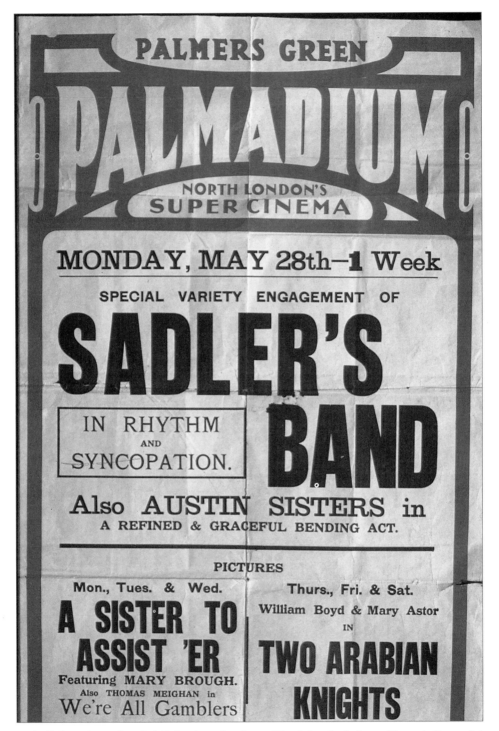

I was thrilled to obtain this playbill for the Palmadium, 'North London's Super Cinema'. Research has revealed that the year is 1928. In this pre-talkies era, the cinema was still offering a stage show, in addition to its silent films. The Palmadium opened on Christmas Eve 1920 to much acclaim, being described as 'London's most magnificent picture house'.

The auditorium of the Palmadium. This picture will no doubt bring back memories to many residents. The seating capacity was 2,500 and, originally, the entertainment comprised a stage show and a full orchestra, as well as the films. Note that the accommodation included the stalls, a dress circle and an upper circle as well as the theatre-style boxes. The cinema closed on 25 February 1961.

Green Lanes, with, from right to left, Burton's the tailors, Capon's gents outfitters and the Queens cinema. On the other side of Lodge Drive is the National Westminster Bank with the Palmadium just showing. Burton's was built on the site of the Thatched Cottage in 1938 (now occupied by Westlake's), while the Queens, built in 1912 and rebuilt in 1927, finally closed in 1967. After a spell as a Bingo Hall, it was demolished in 1971.

Evans & Davies, Palmers Green's premier store, stands out here. Opposite are the premises referred to in the previous picture. Mr Evans and Mr Davies opened a small shop here in 1911 and it was so successful that it grew into a major store, with twenty-seven departments and a lift to all floors. It set the standard for others to follow. Sadly, in post war years, with the profusion of new shopping centres, the store was forced to close.

Looking north from the Triangle, *c*. 1880. A delightful scene showing the old Thatched Cottage on the right. Built in about 1790 by Thomas Lewis, Governor of the Bank of England, as a lodge to a larger house, it became one of the great survivors. Many artists captured the scene and tourists would make a pilgrimage to admire its beauty. It was given a new lease of life as a florist's, before its final demise in 1938.

The Triangle looking north, 1926. The first bus is a London General Omnibus Company vehicle on route 29 from Southgate to Wood Green and Victoria (note the open top) followed by a Dennis single-decker Admiral bus run by Mr A.T. Bennett. These were the great days of the independent operators who competed fiercely with the LGOC.

Looking due south, the flag flies high above the Cock Inn with the 'new' Broadway parade of shops on the right. The inn's stables project towards the roadway with a row of dwellings, including McIntosh's smithy (The Cock Forge) spanning what is now the North Circular Road. It is a peaceful scene, with no traffic to jar our senses.

The Cock Inn (since renamed The Manhattan) is very much part of Palmers Green's history and is thought to date from the fifteenth century. It was set well back from the road, with a large forecourt to accommodate the horse-drawn carriages. There was countryside all around when the inn was kept for more than fifty years by three dear maiden ladies, the Sanderson sisters. The inn was rebuilt in 1885 (as seen here).

At the turn of the century, roller skating had become a popular pastime. John C. Hill, a speculative builder, turned his attention to the construction of Rosalie Skating Rink in Regents Avenue. It opened on 1 October 1910 to great acclaim, with 700 skaters in attendance, but the support soon dwindled and the hall was sold in 1912 to the LGOC as a bus garage.

This print comes from the sale documents of the Bowes Manor estate and shows boating on the lake within the grounds. The lake was, in fact, a cut-off loop of the New River. The manor had an idyllic setting surrounded by parkland with an abundance of trees. In the days of Lord and Lady Truro in the mid-nineteenth century, lavish garden parties were held here.

Palmerston Road was once an integral part of the Bowes Manor estate and had close connections with the manor's last owner, Alderman Sidney. He lived there with his family for thirty-four years before his death in 1889. The road was a private tree-lined avenue, with a gateway at each end, when Sidney built some fine large houses on the New River side. After his death, the estate was sold and development ensued.

Before the North Circular Road was constructed in the late 1920s, Tile Kiln Lane (known today as Tottenhall Road) was an important link with Edmonton to the east. Between Eley's Farm and Pymmes Brook stood the toll gate guarding what is thought to have been the last toll road to survive in north London. It finally disappeared in 1927.

On its way eastwards, Tile Kiln Lane meandered down to Pymmes Brook, crossing by means of a very pretty watersplash and footbridge for the pedestrians and cyclists. It was a favourite beauty spot, with glorious countryside all around.

We are straying into Edmonton territory now, but continuing our journey eastwards down Tile Kiln Lane one path would have taken us to Wyer or Weir Hall. This old print shows the original mansion, demolished in 1818. Mr Sage, shopfitter, then built his own version, a large twin-turreted affair that became a college for young gentlemen. Set in most beautiful grounds, it yielded to the new road network of the 1930s.

At the turn of the century, the halcyon days of Bowes Manor had drawn to a close, and soon Green Lanes would be green no longer. New roads and housing were to spread on either side of the main road, with estate offices set up to attract new residents. Goring's advertise their artistic villas in Upsdell Avenue, though 'one minute from Palmers Green station' seems an optimistic assessment.

CHAPTER SIX

PALMERS GREEN

PART THREE: BOWES ROAD TO THE TRIANGLE

We start our journey in Bowes Road, once called Cock Lane, and work our way up Powys Lane into Broomfield Park. We view Broomfield House, once very much the centre and focal point for Southgate's affairs and celebrations, before crossing over into Aldermans Hill. We discuss Sir William Curtis (1752–1829), who once lived here in his house called Cullands Grove, before returning to the Triangle, with a last nostalgic glance at Green Lanes.

I should explain that Northolme today is 171 Bowes Road and this glorious view taken from the upstairs bedroom in 1914 has a very different aspect today. Then, these grounds were still part of the Arnos Grove estate. Today the view would include the Jehovah's Witnesses' Hall (once the Ritz cinema) and the adjacent shops. Furthermore, today's incessant traffic seems at odds with this peaceful scene of another era.

The grand opening of the Ritz in Bowes Road took place on 21 December 1933. It was a spacious cinema with a large stage and an auditorium holding 2,000 patrons. Externally, the front facade was quite plain, with some unusual arched openings at high level. These were the great days of the cinema but, by the 1960s, many were struggling to survive and closure came in 1974. Today, the building serves as a meeting place for Jehovah's Witnesses.

As the whole area started to develop, with an inflow of new residents, there was pressure on the authorities to provide sufficient school places. Here, members of the Edmonton School Board attend the opening of Bowes Road School in 1901. The school survives to this day, but the quiet lane fronting the building has become a very busy traffic route.

Small local dairies were a feature of life in years gone by, and Manley's Dairy was based on the corner of Bowes Road and Warwick Road, with horse-drawn carts distributing supplies over a wide area. On the back of this postcard, E.T. Manley describes himself as 'Cow Keeper & Dairy Farmer' and lists the prices of all his dairy produce. The building is still recognisable today, the corner shop being occupied by the North London Insurance Group.

The watersplash in Powys Lane, looking north, 1903. We are unaware of Pymmes Brook today as we cross the road bridge (built in 1907) in our cars but, before the development, this was a popular beauty spot. The brook made an ideal meeting place surrounded, as it was, on all sides by the most delightful countryside.

The old entrance gateway to Broomfield. Some historians suggest that, centuries ago, Broomfield House might have been used as a hunting lodge and that the hooks inside the gateway, beneath the arch, served to suspend and display the trophies of the hunt. The archway still survives, with the climbing greenery much reduced over the passage of time.

Broomfield House has been much photographed through the years and the pictures reveal the many changes. This old scene, before the mock timbering was applied, reveals its quiet beauty. With the departure of Sir Ralph Littler and the subsequent opening of Broomfield Park in 1903, the house became a focal point for the borough, sadly interrupted by the fire of 1984.

This shows the lawns at the rear of Broomfield House. Though the picture is undated, the fashions tell of another era. The opening of the Museum in 1925 created further interest. Many celebrations, both of local and national events, have been held in the park throughout its history, including those involving wartime rallies and anniversaries.

Alderman Sir William Curtis was an extraordinary, if controversial, character. Born in 1752, son of a ship's biscuit maker in Wapping, he rapidly climbed the social, commercial and political ladders, making friends (and some enemies) on the way. He became a staunch Tory MP and was much pilloried by his political opponents for his alleged illiteracy and obesity. His energy led him down many paths and a large turn-out attended his funeral in 1829.

Sir William Curtis' home was here at Cullands Grove in Aldermans Hill, so named after his appointment as alderman at the early age of thirty-three. The house was set in the attractive grounds of the Old Park estate. The lavish parties held here became legendary, very often with royalty in attendance. J.D. Taylor bought the whole estate and demolished the house in 1840.

Looking west up Aldermans Hill and featuring the 'Long Pond', left, almost opposite the Derwent Road of today. The pond was accessible from the roadway at either end and it was normal practice to allow the horses and carriages to splash their way through, to cool off on a hot summer's day. The pond disappeared when the Old Park estate was developed.

Aldermans Hill in 1896, looking east towards the railway bridge and Palmers Green station. The railway had already been in operation for some twenty-five years, but its effects were slow to materialise. There is gas lighting, but there are no kerbstones or proper pavements. The road surface remains substantial enough to cope with the occasional horsebus on its way to the station.

This delightful residence, Old Park House, was built for Colin Docwra, son of Thomas Docwra of Swanage who, in 1833, founded a well-known firm of public works contractors. It stood in extensive grounds, just east of the Old Park Road junction of today. Subsequent owners included the May family and Thomas Melville, a highly respected local councillor. It was demolished in the mid-1930s.

Looking north from the Triangle up Green Lanes, 1880. The Thatched Cottage, on the far side, displays its old-world charm. On the left we can see the front garden walls of some dwellings, where the bank is today. This quiet scene reminds us of village life, long before the creation of a busy suburb.

Though the traffic is minimal, this picture of the Triangle in the 1930s shows some activity with the policeman on duty. Note the fine Midland Bank building facing us on the left (well maintained and looking as pristine today) and, just three doors away, the gable-roofed premises which many residents will remember as one of Sainsbury's branches.

It is Coronation Day, 12 May 1937, and the Triangle is bedecked with flags, showing Palmers Green in all its glory. The trams are still running and the Queens and Palmadium cinemas are playing to packed houses. The shops, too, are well decorated, in particular the Evans & Davies store.

The author has fond memories of the old cinemas in the borough, not least the Palmadium (see also pages 61 and 62). It was a magnificent building, with stage shows and a full orchestra supplementing the silent films, when it opened in 1920. The 'Palm Court' attached was used as a British Restaurant during the Second World War. Demolished in 1961, the site has been developed with a parade of shops, which includes a Tesco supermarket.

The caption on this postcard says it all.

C H A P T E R   S E V E N

WINCHMORE HILL

P A R T   O N E :   B O U R N E   H I L L   T O   T H E   G R E E N

In olden times, we could climb the stile in Dog & Duck Lane (now Bourne Hill) and stroll down a footpath (now Broad Walk) through the enchanting Winchmore Hill Woods on our way to the Green. We could make a detour into Mr Taylor's Grovelands estate, still marked as Deer Park on the 1897 OS map. At the end of the footpath lay Winchmore Hill Green, the heart of the old village.

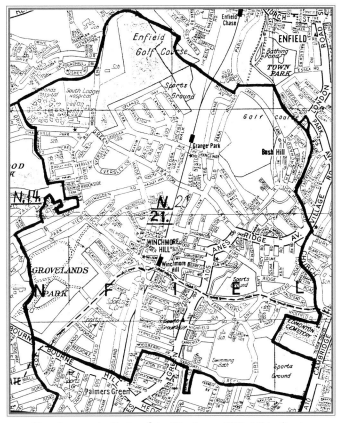

Map showing the limits of the Winchmore Hill, N21, district.

The Keeper's Cottage, home to Mr Taylor's gamekeeper, was delightfully situated close to the footpath that led from Dog & Duck Lane, through Winchmore Hill Woods, towards the Green. It was an idyllic walk for the villagers, particularly in spring and summer. The site today is occupied by White Timbers in Broad Walk, opposite the Brackendale turning.

This photograph was taken by Henrietta Cresswell in 1889. It depicts the footpath through the woods, looking towards the Green. As a young girl Henrietta, daughter of Dr John Cresswell, played in these woods with her friends and writes of the magical atmosphere of these awe-inspiring surroundings.

The making of charcoal dates back to the thirteenth century and is one of the oldest trades of the village. Areas were designated as coppice wood and the trees were then cut methodically, in rotation, every ten years. Some of the timber was used for fuel and the bark was peeled and sent to the nearby tanneries. The skill of the 'colyers' who camped in the woods was paramount in the production of high grade charcoal.

Clamps would be formed by propping the cut timbers around a central pole, creating an igloo-shaped enclosure, which would then be fired. The clamp would be covered with mould and leaves to ensure a slow and steady burn (seven to ten days and nights), essential for good quality charcoal, once a very important fuel in this country.

On 9 June 1902, the Taylor estates in their entirety were put on the market. The bidding for Lot No. 9 (the Grovelands estate) did not reach the reserve price and, when Captain Taylor and his wife returned from honeymoon in 1903, they were able to return to the old family home. They are seen here being welcomed by all the staff on their arrival.

Grovelands Park was opened on 12 April 1913 and has given enjoyment and recreation to thousands. What is better than a brisk walk around the lake on a nice sunny day? The author remembers when the rowing boats could still be hired for a trip around the island with one's school chums on board. Happy days!

On our way to Winchmore Hill Green, there is a clearing in the wood and a pathway widens to reveal this delightful scene.

We approach the edge of the wood and look back along the footpath. Before the establishment of our local churches, the villagers would have made this pilgrimage: out on to the Green; down Middle Lane (Station Road); across a very leafy Green Lanes into Fords Grove; along the Hyde footpath into Church Street, thus reaching their destination, All Saints in Edmonton.

Our journey along the footpath to the Green terminates at Mummery's. You can see the footpath just to the left of the shop, which fronted a few cottages known as Wood Corner, demolished around 1912. Previously this shop had traded as Udall & Childs, an establishment of great renown, whose customers included the well-to-do from miles around.

Originally Rowantree and Woodside, right, were one house called Woodside, thought to be at least 250 years old. The cottages adjacent were extended to form a shop in about 1840. Mr G. Richards, a draper, traded there for many years, followed by Mably's, well remembered by many and pictured here in 1955. The premises currently serve as a dental surgery.

Tidey's or Dicky Bird corner was a cherished feature of the old village. The corner shop was originally called Tidey's, which became the newsagent's just round the corner in Hoppers Road and the corner sweet shop was renamed Dicky Bird. There was an old-world charm about them and locals were saddened at the demolition of the whole corner in 1965.

Compare Dicky Bird corner after demolition with the one above and we realise it left a scar, slow to heal. The whole corner site is currently (1998) being redeveloped, with everyone's hope that the new will blend in well with the surroundings.

Winchmore Hill Green looking east towards Station Road, showing the entrance to Roseville, remembered by many as a doctor's home and surgery. Roseville's history goes back to the late eighteenth century, when it was part of a much larger estate. John Ashley, an official of the Great Northern Railway, lived here during the construction of the railway.

Roseville was a rather plain ashlar-faced, flat-topped building of three storeys. From 1889 to 1921 it was occupied by Dr R.T. Vivian and his wife, who had three doctor sons. It later became the home and surgery of Dr Gordon Simpson and his wife Edith, fondly remembered by many.

A rare photograph of the old original village inn, the Kings Head. It is likely that it started life as two dwellings, with the portico entrance added later. It faced on to Wades Hill with a tiny garden and a picket fence, but the main gardens, a delight in summer, were across the way. The present Kings Head & Railway Hotel, built in 1896, bears no resemblance to the old.

Winchmore Hill Green in years gone by, with the cab rank and horse trough just visible on the right. We can also see the familiar curve of the shopping parade and the Kings Head in the distance, with not a car in sight.

The smithy which once lay behind what is now the Regatta restaurant. The horses would be led down the passageway, now guarded by a door, to be shod, while the owners washed their carts in the village pond. This photograph is dated 1933, though the smithy ceased to function in the 1920s.

The village bakery dates back to about 1720 and was run in recent times by the Chalkley family. Though the premises are now a private residence, evidence of their original purpose remains. The loading-bay door on the south side survives and the alley leads to the old stables. The ovens ceased to operate in about 1945, though the corner shop continued into the 1960s.

The triangle of green and the horse chestnut tree, where Compton Road joins Hoppers Road, still survive. We can see the original version of the Salisbury Arms, nearer to the Green than its modern counterpart, which replaced it in 1935. On the extreme left are the railings of Belmont House, which served for a time as a girls' school.

A lovely scene looking due south down Hoppers Road. The triangle and tree are just visible together with Taylor's Cottages and Belmont House, now the site of the Salisbury Arms. The old cottages in the distance have long since disappeared.

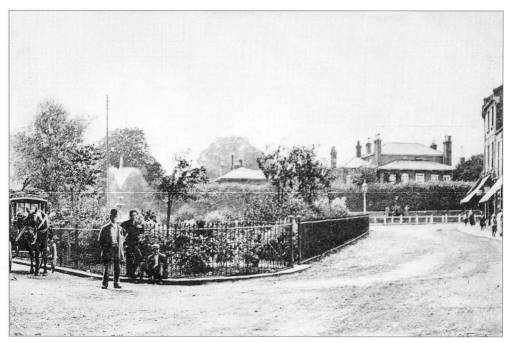

Earlier this century, the west side of the Green featured two houses. The Limes stood facing the Green near the junction with Broad Walk, prior to demolition in 1955. Uplands, distant right, was a very large house which made way for flats in 1934. Note the railings around the Green and the fountain.

A rare picture showing the large pond on the Green, which survived until 1908, when filled in by the Council. The shops, left, were built on what had been a very colourful front garden belonging to the village bakery.

CHAPTER EIGHT

WINCHMORE HILL

PART TWO: ALL ROADS LEAD TO THE KINGS HEAD

This section deals with the roads on the west side of Green Lanes, many of which radiate from, or are fairly adjacent to, the Green. These include Church Hill, Eversley Park Road, Green Dragon Lane, Worlds End Lane, Wades Hill, Vicars Moor Lane and Station Road. As the old villagers used to say, 'all roads lead uphill to the Kings Head'.

Phillips the butcher and the adjoining cottages in Church Hill, 1938. On the extreme right, we can just see the railings of Devon House. The meat was supplied from local farms, and the slaughterhouse, originally in a covered yard at the side of the shop, was later rebuilt at the rear. This photograph was taken shortly before demolition.

Laurel Lodge in Church Hill, seen here in 1955, was built by Thomas Mann for his son Edward. When his mother died in the 1890s, Sir Edward moved to Roseneath and various notables subsequently lived here. Later known as The Laurels, many will remember it as The Chesterfield Club in the 1950s, prior to demolition.

Some of the old cottages in Church Hill still survive to remind us of the origins of our village but this one, Ivy Cottage, has yielded to the developers. It was situated just below the church, on the south side of the hill.

This imposing mansion, Stone Hall, was built in 1872 and stood in extensive grounds, almost opposite St Paul's Church. It was built for Alfred Walker, proprietor of Stone's Ginger Wine and then, in 1885, Clare Regnart took possession. The estate was sold in 1932–3 for redevelopment and only the lodge remains. This photograph dates from April 1933.

Apart from being an imposing residence, Stone Hall served as a successful, productive dairy farm, with grazing for a large herd of Jerseys. These were the attractive stables, built within the grounds, and again, photographed in April 1933.

Looking up Church Hill towards the Green, 1886. Winchmore Hill remains a quiet, sleepy village. The land to the right was then owned by the Taylors, while the left-hand side lies undeveloped. There are no proper pavements and the roads are free of traffic.

These large and impressive, well-built houses stood in Church Hill between the Stone Hall and Houndsden Road turnings, but few remain. Those pictured above have been demolished to make way for flats (Chesterfield Lodge).

This view is undated but shows a very rural scene. We are looking into the dip of Eversley Park Road towards the Chase Side Tavern (currently renamed The Winchmore Arms). Perhaps the children are on their way to school.

This photograph is dated November 1930 and shows the countryside in the vicinity of what is now Hadley Way. We are looking due east and can just identify the railway embankment, right, on the approach to Grange Park station.

A classic view of olden times in Green Dragon Lane. It is a completely rural scene of trees, hedges and fields, with just a track for the roadway. Mum goes ahead with the pram, while the two children, with their dog, pause to pose for the camera.

Although the railway had arrived in 1871 – note the bridge in the far distance – the scene in Green Dragon Lane remained completely rural half a century later. We can just identify Filcaps Farm on the left, the point at which Landra Gardens joins today. We are looking east towards Masons Corner and hedgerows and trees abound.

The entrance to the Northern Hospital was just inside Worlds End Lane. It was built in 1886 and used then for fever and convalescent cases. Built on a 36½ acre site, there were nineteen separate pavilions with nearly 800 beds. It became a District General Hospital, was renamed Highlands in 1948, and merged with the hospital next door, South Lodge, in 1966. The closure came in the mid-1990s when a major building programme commenced.

The transformation of Worlds End Lane in modern times has been staggering. The lane was aptly named. Originally it simply led to a hollow by the side of a stream. All around was open countryside, as this picture dated 1935 illustrates. With the modern development of schools and housing, the Highlands development and the growth of traffic, the change has been quite dramatic.

Some parts of the old village have not changed so much. We are in Wades Hill looking south towards the Green. The clapboarded cottages will be familiar and many of us will remember Knowles' cycle shop on the corner with Wades Grove. Once again the lack of traffic highlights the main difference from today.

These Esther Doe Almshouses in Wades Hill were erected in 1868 for '12 spinsters of limited means and incapable of earning a living'. They were financed by Esther Doe in memory of her husband and her father, but were demolished in 1974 to make way for the new accommodation built on the corner of Paulin Drive.

The marriage of William Paulin and Fanny Mann was a happy alliance and they came to be known as Lord and Lady Bountiful, so great was their kindness to the village. Their eldest daughter, Ina, married Revd Arthur Dewdney, Minister of St Paul's, and the younger, Irene, seen here in pony and trap outside the family home, Broadfields, proved to be a tower of strength after the death of her father in 1931.

The view is Wades Hill, looking north, in 1929. The railings guard the stream known as Hounsden Gutter and in the distance the hill climbs towards Green Dragon Lane. The developers wasted no time – by 1933 the fields and trees were just a memory.

Rose Cottage was once the home of Thomas Hood (1799–1845), renowned poet and humorist of Scottish descent (see inset). The plaque on 59 Vicars Moor Lane today identifies the site. Thomas was a frequent visitor to the Lamb household in Enfield. Rose Cottage was demolished following bomb damage during the Second World War.

Roseneath in Vicars Moor Lane was set in beautiful grounds, and it was here, in 1871, that Thomas Mann set up the Winchmore Hill Village Cricket and Lawn Tennis Club, with W.G. Grace making an occasional appearance. Thomas' son, Sir Edward, lived at Roseneath until 1913. It was used as a hospital for wounded soldiers during the First World War and later as a private nursing home. The photograph is dated 1920.

Another view that is difficult to recognise today, so vast have been the changes. From the railway embankment near Grange Park station, we look across the beautiful countryside to witness the early days of house building along The Chine and Old Park Ridings. The building of the station in 1910 prompted the development. Interrupted by the war, the expansion continued and the countryside became a memory.

Winchmore Hill station. The railway arrived in 1871, but the immediate effect was far from dramatic. The horsebuses into town were fewer, as they could now concentrate on serving the new stations. It signified the start of improved communication with the metropolis, which set in motion the expansion that was to follow in the next century.

Although the station opened in 1871, it was not until 1900 that Middle Lane officially became Station Road. Some of these shops can be quite easily identified today, though the villagers strolling in the middle of the road suggest another era. The shop premises on the right, now demolished, served as a barber's shop during its latter years.

St Paul's Institute was built in 1903 by William Paulin as the new Parish Hall, in memory of his wife Fanny. It lasted for over sixty years and served a multiplicity of purposes during that time. It will be remembered by many for the popular dances held here, particularly during wartime. It was demolished to make way for the new GPO District Sorting Office.

CHAPTER NINE

WINCHMORE HILL

PART THREE: ALONG GREEN LANES AND BEYOND

We travel north along Green Lanes, originally a drover's track but now a major artery with a constant flow of traffic. We look at the development of the Broadway following the extension of the tramway from Manor House, and progress to Bush Hill and St Stephen's Church. The section closes with a glance at the eastern side of the parish, perhaps the last to submit to the spread of suburbia.

Once part of Highfield Park, St Bartholomew's Sports Ground opened in 1895. It was a superb ground, up to county standard, with a fine pavilion. During the Second World War, it was used by Stationers' School. In the early 1990s, after some controversy, it was developed as a huge Sainsbury supermarket with a large car park completely filling the site.

Holy Trinity was built in 1908, to serve a growing population on the eastern side of the parish, following the arrival of the trams. The Revd Arthur Dewdney of St Paul's was instrumental in helping to raise funds. Badly damaged by fire in 1978, the church has been fully restored, with some radical alterations.

The trams are running down Winchmore Hill Broadway and the shops are in their heyday. The tramway was extended from Manor House and reached the Green Dragon in 1907. This triggered a rapid development of housing, schools, churches and shops. The trams survived until 1938, when replaced by the trolleybuses.

The shops on the west side of Winchmore Hill Broadway were built in 1904–5. The announcement had already been made that the trams were on their way and the developers wasted no time. Sainsbury was an early starter (1905) and this well-remembered branch gave great service, closing in 1973. Nearly twenty years later, the supermarket opened and the original shop has become a pub.

A typical Sainsbury's shop interior, with its central entrance doors, the tiled walls and counter upstands, the marble shelves and the attractive black and white tessellated floor. Everything was clean and spotless. There were chairs to rest awhile and the cash desk, where customers settled their account, was at the end.

In the early years of development, there was great competition between the electricity and gas industries to capture the market. These gas showrooms opened in 1911 and gave great service, until recent years, when policy dictated their closure. This photograph shows the fire of 1988, when the premises were trading as an office furniture store.

Private schools were popular early this century and the Winchmore Hill Collegiate School, which opened in 1906, prospered until its closure in 1963. It was situated at the top of Farm Road, adjacent to the New River, with the headmaster's house adjoining.

Southgate escaped the wholesale devastation that some areas experienced during the Blitz. Nevertheless, there were many incidents to remind us of the horrors of war. This HE bomb fell in Green Lanes opposite the Capitol cinema at 3.45 a.m. on 9 October 1940, when several houses were destroyed, with serious loss of life.

The Shrubbery was a lovely old house set in several acres of grounds, on the west side of Green Lanes, just before Vicars Moor Lane. Miraculously, it has survived, though in a completely different form. In 1926–7 the house was incorporated in the parade of shops and is today (1998) the Dragon Garden Chinese Restaurant and Stern's the chemist. This photograph shows the south facing or garden front, now built on.

Looking east down Firs Lane with the Gibraltar Cottages, built in the 1780s, on the corner with Green Lanes to our left. The site is now occupied by the Telephone Exchange, but previously the area had connections with brick and tile making. The cottages were built by John Blackburn, a major landowner, who lived at Bush Hill House.

This print of Old Park, one of the prestigious houses in the area, is dated 1730. It is now the home of Bush Hill Park Golf Club. The last private owner was John Walker Ford, who carried out considerable enlargement to the property. The grounds were leased to the golf club in 1912, and the house used as its headquarters from 1920.

The Clarendon Arch was rebuilt in 1682, to replace the old bridge in Bush Hill. The archway supports the road and originally carried the waters of Salmons Brook eastwards under both the roadway and the New River. In post-war years, to obviate flooding, the archway has been effectively replaced and the brook is now culverted in a massive concrete circular ducting, some 7 ft in diameter.

> This Bank of Earth was raised and formed
> to support the Channel of the New River.
> And the Frame of timber and lead,
> which served that purpose 173 Years
> was removed and taken away.
> MDCCLXXXVI.
> PETER HOLFORD Esquire
> GOVERNOR.

MDCCLXXXVI translates to 1786. If we take away the 173 years, as the inscription instructs, we arrive at 1613. The New River was a marvellous conception carried out from 1609 to 1613 under the control of Sir Hugh Myddelton. The construction of the huge aqueduct required at this point was a great engineering feat.

Ridge Road was once part of a delightful walk the villagers would make on their way to Edmonton. A detour off Firs Lane would lead us on through glorious countryside to Church Street and All Saints. It was originally called Jews Corner Lane, Jews Corner being a beauty spot where the Ridge Road of today joins Church Street.

In 1907 the tramway extension from Manor House to Winchmore Hill was opened. The 'end of the ride' then was the Green Dragon. The extension to Enfield Town was a tremendous feat of engineering for it required not only laying the tracks, but also widening the road in many areas. A new road had to be constructed through the Red Ridge estate (Ridge Avenue) before the first tram, seen here, could arrive at Enfield, July 1909.

There were wild scenes as the last tram completed its journey in May 1938, to coincide the following morning with the introduction of the trolleybuses, the first of which is seen here at Enfield Town bound for Tottenham Court Road. The 'trolleys' had some shortcomings, but many advantages and benefits, for, in today's parlance, they were 'environmentally friendly'.

The 'Iron Church' of St Stephen's was built in 1901, and the scene was still completely rural. When the new church was consecrated in 1907, this building acted as the church hall, prior to its demolition in 1925. It had the reputation of being like an oven in summer, and an ice box in winter.

The building of St Stephen's Church continued in stages and, in spite of the war, reached completion on 17 November 1915. This picture, dated 1928, shows the magnificence of the church with its lychgate (1922) and the new hall, just to the north, which opened in 1926.

This picture shows the cottages on the north side of Highfield Road, as we look due east up to the humpback bridge over the New River. Before the cottages were built, in about 1875, a clear stream ran its course here with a profusion of wild flowers. The tiny shop, left of the bridge, was once Gandy's, which evokes special memories of an old-fashioned shop that sold everything.

This is a very early view of Highfield Row, as it was called then, looking west, with the old Orange Tree on the right. It was a very irregular track with another old alehouse, the Moulders Arms, projecting into the roadway. It remained a quiet backwater well into the 1900s.

The 'red tin hut' which stood in Highfield Road next to the school. In the 1890s an appeal was made to the Vicar of St Paul's for a house of worship on the eastern side of the parish and, consequently, this corrugated iron chapel was built. Once Holy Trinity was opened in 1908 to satisfy a growing population, the hut was used for many years for social events, prior to demolition.

Farming was the main occupation for the villagers before the arrival of suburbia and here is another example, Fords Grove Farm, which stood on the south side of Farm Road with extensive acreage all around. The clapboarded construction and tiny porchway at the entrance are typical of the period.

It is little wonder that Fords Grove, seen here, was a popular walk for the villagers. They could continue along the Hyde footpath (Firs Park Avenue), through an area rich in nurseries and greenhouses, on their way to Edmonton.

CHAPTER TEN

AROUND & ABOUT

This final section gives me licence to include some pictures of special interest to me and I hope to you, the reader. On occasion I have strayed beyond the borders. Transport, entertainment and the wartime are just some of the topics briefly touched on. Please excuse my indulgence.

Temple Bar was the gateway in the Strand, between the cities of London and Westminster. Built to the design of Sir Christopher Wren in 1672, it replaced an old gate that previously marked this spot. It caused severe hindrance to traffic and was dismantled in 1878 and stored for ten years. Sir Henry and Lady Meux then had it re-erected stone by stone, to form an imposing entrance to their estate at Theobalds. A lodge was added, left, to house the gatekeeper.

This postcard is postmarked 1905 and shows Friern Barnet Road looking east towards the junction with Bowes Road and Waterfall Lane. Station Road joins from the right, with the bank on the corner (now a pub, The Bankers Draft) and The Turrets to our left. The scene is recognisable today except that modern traffic usually clogs this road in both directions.

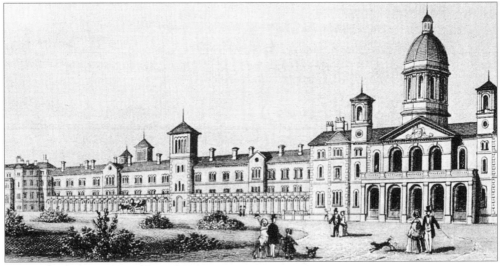

The Colney Hatch Asylum was opened in 1851, when it housed 1,250 patients. It later expanded to serve more than twice this number. It was in close proximity to the Great Northern Railway and had its own station. It was a new conception, designed to make the inmates fulfil a useful role and be self-supporting. It would take the visitor more than five hours to walk the wards. The hospital's policies were more liberal and humane than ever before. In 1959 it was renamed Friern Hospital. In 1983 policy dictated that patients be treated 'within the community' and closure came on 31 March 1993.

The Edmonton Volunteer Fire Brigade of 1882. The picture illustrates the great difficulties that existed before motorisation and the sophisticated equipment we take for granted today. In an emergency, the volunteers were called out and dispatched to the fire by horse-drawn tender, where water was seldom readily available. In a service where speed is the essence, there were, of course, great limitations.

Enfield was once renowned for its brick making. The brickfields were numerous, mostly situated around the Lea valley, where the brick earth was ideal material and where barge traffic was available for transportation into the capital. Many skills and traditions were involved, but the industry slowly petered out, as the land became more valuable for urban development.

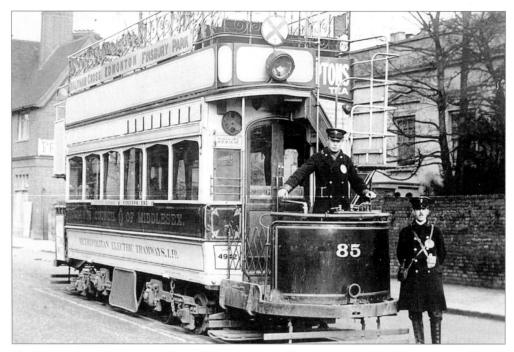

The driver and conductor pose in front of their tram at Waltham Cross, *c.* 1910. This service ran through Edmonton and Tottenham via Hertford Road and Fore Street, and on to Finsbury Park. The Lipton advertisement can be seen, partially obscured.

Two trams rest awhile at the Enfield terminus outside The George, *c.* 1920. Note the Pearson Bros sign in the background. Note the open-top tram standing alongside a more modern closed-top vehicle. Power was picked up from the overhead lines. It seems Sir Thomas Lipton had commandeered all available space for advertising his shops.

The London General Omnibus Company faced stiff and unyielding competition from the independent or 'pirate' bus companies during the 1920s. One of the most famous was the popular navy-blue Admiral fleet, set up by a local man, Bernard Cosgrove, and later taken over by Alfred Bennett, a giant among the independent bus operators. He lived for most of his life in Green Dragon Lane.

The arrival of the trams in 1907 accelerated development all along, and either side of, the Green Lanes route, but it was not until 1912 that the motor bus service No. 29 reached Southgate. This splendid bus at the Cherry Tree in 1949 bears little resemblance to the original solid tyre version.

This delightful picture shows Cock Hill, looking due south towards the Chase Side Tavern, *c.* 1895. It was later renamed Eversley Park Road and an entrance gate into the Eversley estate can be seen, left of picture. It was just a country lane with no pavements or lighting. To the right is the valley of the Hounsden Gutter, where much of the land formed part of Home Farm, owned by the Taylors.

This photograph of Green Lanes, Palmers Green, looking north is undated, but guesswork suggests the 1920s. The two schoolboys, extreme right, are doubtless from Southgate County School in Fox Lane (the author's old school). Other points of interest include the approaching tram and overhead wires, the cars, the bank, the Palmadium cinema and the general air of hustle and bustle.

The Regal cinema, on the corner of Silver Street and Fore Street in Edmonton, was one built in the grand manner in 1934, with a certain opulence in its design. Three thousand patrons could be accommodated and no expense was spared in its general decor. By the 1960s audiences had started to dwindle. It closed in 1972, but survived as a bingo hall for a while. The final rites came in 1986 with demolition and the building of a supermarket.

The Savoy cinema in Southbury Road, Enfield, opened its doors in October 1935, when the film show was augmented by a stage presentation. Its outside appearance was modest in comparison with the Regal but the auditorium, seen here, had a classic Art Deco style. It had close links with the ABC chain, which Cannon bought in 1985, when it was renamed accordingly. Amid controversy, closure came in 1997 to make way for a new supermarket.

We stay in Enfield to look at two delightful inns in Clay Hill. The Rose & Crown has been much photographed through the years nestling, as it does, in a little hollow close by Hilly Fields. There are connections with Dick Turpin whose grandfather, Mr Nott, was once the licensee here. Turpin's hideouts are said to have included the old Queens Head in Winchmore Hill.

The Fallow Buck is perched on the crest of Clay Hill, right on the eastern boundary of what was formerly Enfield Chase. This lovely old clapboarded house first traded as an inn 280 years ago and thankfully has maintained its character and purpose into modern times.

In the very early years of aviation history, the landing of this aircraft in Pymmes Park, in July 1912, caused a sensation. The young pilot by the name of Astley was returning to Hendon but, running short of petrol, was forced to land. A large crowd saw him take off the following morning. Mr Astley, sadly, met with a fatal accident just two months later.

E.A. (Gussie) Bowles (1865–1954) was one of the great gardeners of the twentieth century. His love of horticulture led him to explore many foreign climes and introduce several new species here. A fine artist and a man of many talents, Gussie Bowles lived at Myddelton House in Bulls Cross, where recent endeavours have helped to restore the gardens to their former splendour.

The original Selborne Hall was built on the site of the outdoor skittles alley of the Cherry Tree inn. In 1956–7 major improvements were carried out to the inn, and particularly to the hall, including extensions, a car park and a sunken garden. The new version, above, became a popular venue for dinner dances but, in December 1996, together with changes to the inn (now a Big Steak House), Selborne Hall was converted into a Wacky Warehouse.

History is not just about the dim and distant past. Local residents who are now of senior status will have their own memories of the Blitz and the trials and tribulations of the Second World War. This bomb destroyed a house in Queen Elizabeth Drive in 1940 and damaged neighbouring properties.

There are many famous people from all walks of life who have had connections with this area, and I close my book with just one example. Dame Flora Robson (1902–84), distinguished actress, grew up in the family home at 65 The Mall. Her parents were very much involved with the setting up of the Congregational Church in Fox Lane, where a young Flora performed in concert parties. She initially attended Miss Hum's school, before transferring to Palmers Green High School in Hoppers Road. She was indeed very proud of her connections with the old Borough of Southgate.

INDEX